The FIREPLACE BOOK *Volume 2*

AN IDEA BOOK OF FIREPLACE DESIGNS

by the editors of Aberdeen's Magazine of Masonry Construction

The FIREPLACE BOOK *Volume 2*

AN IDEA BOOK OF FIREPLACE DESIGNS

by the editors of Aberdeen's Magazine of Masonry Construction

The Aberdeen Group®

426 S. Westgate St., Addison, Illinois 60101
Telephone: 708-543-0870 Fax: 708.543.3112

CONTENTS

OTHER ABERDEEN GROUP BOOKS OF INTEREST

- The Fireplace Book, Volume 1

- Masonry Repair and Restoration:
  A Guide to Techniques and Materials

- Mortar: How to Specify and Use
  Masonry Mortar

- Masonry Inspection and Maintenance:
  Troubleshooting and Preserving
  Masonry Structures

- Nondestructive Evaluation & Testing
  of Masonry Structures

WELCOME TO
The FIREPLACE
BOOK *Volume 2*

Building or remodeling your home is an exciting experience, but it can present you with an intimidating array of choices. Few of those choices can affect the value, comfort, and enjoyment of your home as strongly as the fireplace.

Three years ago, we published The Fireplace Book. Its goal was to make choosing masonry fireplaces a little easier, while giving readers an idea of the options available to them. The response to the first book was immediate and gratifying. Within weeks of its publication, people started asking for more. So here is Volume II, an all-new collection of photographs to help you, your architect, your builder, and your masonry contractor come up with a fireplace design that exactly suits your home and lifestyle.

Why choose masonry?

An all-masonry fireplace, properly constructed with a firebrick firebox, a clay flue liner, and a face and chimney of brick, concrete block, or stone, is the traditional first choice for many reasons. Masonry is the most durable material you can use. It adds the most to a home's resale value and, in some areas, reduces insurance rates. And if offers the greatest variety of sizes, shapes, colors, and textures to help you make a unique architectural statement.

Factors to consider

When planning your fireplace, consider all these points:

- **Size.** How large are the room and the wall where the fireplace will be located? Your fireplace should be large enough to serve as a focal point, but not so big that it overwhelms the space. Firebox size also is important. Too large a fire can make a small room uncomfortably warm. Too small a fire may not create the atmosphere you want.
- **Heat.** How much will you rely on the fireplace to heat the space? If you want the fireplace to be a supplemental heat source, then incorporate a heat circulation system into the design or consider a Rumford style (page 37) or a masonry heater (page 43). These units take full advantage of masonry's ability to store and radiate heat.
- **Convenience.** How much time and effort will you spend in starting and maintaining a fire? Consider using a gas starter or even a gas log for the greatest ease of operation. Include an ash pit to make cleaning the fireplace neater and easier. Decide whether your fireplace design should include a storage bin for firewood.
- **Style.** The fireplaces in this book (and the first volume) only suggest the range of possibilities. From comfortably rustic to dignified traditional to sleekly contemporary, masonry's variety makes it suitable for any style of architecture and interior design. The range of colors, textures, patterns, and scales offered by brick, concrete block, and natural stone is virtually infinite.
- **Safe, efficient operation.** You'll want your fireplace to burn brightly, draw smoke efficiency up and out the chimney, and minimize any risk of a house or chimney fire. Make sure the design you choose provides for outside air to feed combustion. This is especially important in today's tightly sealed, energy-efficient homes. And make sure the design and construction follow all applicable building and fire code requirements.

A custom-built masonry fireplace can satisfy all these needs and desires. We hope you'll be informed and inspired by the photographs and articles in this book. We expect you'll enjoy your new fireplace for years to come.

Ken Hooker

Ken Hooker
Editor
Magazine of Masonry Construction

Ottavio Rosati

BRICK
FIREPLACES

Because a brick by definition can be held
and placed comfortably with one hand, a
brick fireplace easily provides a comfortable,
domestic scale in the most intimate setting.
But brickwork adapts just as well to grand
designs in monumental spaces.

Even if your budget is tight, you can vary
the color and texture of the brick and mortar,
the bond pattern, and even the position of
units in the wall. By doing so, you can create
an unlimited variety of truly distinctive
designs, while adding little or nothing to the
cost of the project.

Steven Dahill

Steven Dahill

Turba Photography, DePere, WI

Jeffrey Hoffman

Opposite Page, Top, Left and Right The contemporary fireplace accommodates two structural piers added to support a carrying beam installed after the general framing was complete. Since the fireplace had to be stepped out 18 inches while the firebox remained in place, three concentric arches – one header course, one rowlock course, and one soldier course – were added. A center herringbone panel, inset between the two vertical piers, provides an attractive balance to the arch. This fireplace is made of Glen-Gery 5300 Pavers with bluestone hearth and mantel shelf. Designer and masonry contractor: Steven E. Dahill, North East Masonry Associates, Maynard, MA.

Opposite Page, Bottom The unusual stone-like effect of this contemporary floor-to-ceiling fireplace comes from the white, handmade, oversize Lorraine brick from Glen-Gery Corp. The raised hearth and brick mantel shelf add to the design. It pale colors blend in well with a room of big windows and wicker furniture. Masonry contractor: Popp Masonry, Green Bay, WI.

Top This fireplace, with is horizontal lines and traditional flavor, is made of 1776 Danish Brick and a Glen-Gery color mortar blend. Three courses of corbeled brick create a tiered mantle that echoes the raised hearth. Masonry contractor: Welbilt Homes, Mohnton, PA.

Eugene Plueger Masonry Contractor

Opposite Page Two strong vertical piers stand guard for this gray, brick, air-circulating fireplace which reaches to a cathedral ceiling. The curved, raised hearth and wood mantel shelf accent the fireplace. Masonry contractor: Lawrence M. Kowalczyk, Design/Build Concepts Ltd., Mundelein, IL.

Top Triple arches create a dramatic fireplace wall. Made of 8-inch modular brick, it has a centered fireplace, flanked by wood storage areas, a raised hearth, and a recessed oak mantel shelf. An enclosed metal firebox forces heat through the furnace ductwork. Masonry contractor: Eugene Plueger, Eugene Plueger Masonry Contractor, LeMars, IA.

Bottom, Left This brick fireplace has classical overtones thanks to an arched shape that echoes the Palladian windows on either side. The masonry is 8-inch Jamestown Brick in a dark tone that contrasts with the reeded wood mantel shelf and wood insets, all in a warm, honey-pecan finish. Masonry contractor: Scott S. Tiehes, SST Masonry Inc., Raymore MO.

Bottom, Right The mason who built this fireplace describes it as "rustic" and the Glen-Gery 53DD Brick used for the facing and hearth fits that description. But the dark wood mantel shelf, with its triple panel inset, makes the fireplace quite formal as well. It also has strong horizontal lines thanks to the 4-foot-wide opening and brass fire screen. Masonry contractor: Edward J. Zywusko, E-Z Masonry, Beverly, MA.

Stanley Sackett

Stanley Sackett

Edward J. Zywusko

J&M Masonry Inc.

Opposite Page, Top Left and Right Provided the bedroom doors are open, this contemporary fireplace can be seen from every room in the house. The living room face is set at a 45-degree angle to the walls, presenting an angular shape at the point of entry. Made of Cortez brick, including the 45-degree angle brick that permits the one-half bond throughout, this fireplace extends to the 17-foot ceiling. The arched fireplace opening is repeated to top off the vertical running bond over the mantel shelf and the soldiers on the rounded, raised hearth. Designer: Stanley Sackett, Sackett Brick Company, Kalamazoo, MI. Masonry contractor: Joe Haase, Builders Masonry, Galesburg, MI.

Opposite Page, Bottom Used brick creates this rustic-style niche for an iron woodstove. Behind the stove, the brick wall is slanted to reflect more heat into the room. The vertical wood storage area has an arched opening. Architect and masonry contractor: Edward J. Zywusko, E-Z Masonry, Beverly, MA.

Top Strong columns accent the sides of this brick fireplace with its arched opening, oak mantel shelf and raised hearth. Buff mortar is used in raked joints. Set within the two columns, six amber glass blocks are back lit to give a soft glow that echoes the open flame. Architect and masonry contractor: John H. Witzel, Jr., J&M Masonry Inc., Virginia Beach, VA.

Ottavio Rosati

Reuben Etter

Opposite Page In keeping with the traditional post-and-beam construction of this house, the brick fireplace has Early American style. Even the firebox opening is reminiscent of cooking fireplaces in colonial kitchens, and the hewn mantel shelf echoes the beams above it. Designer: G.F Herrman, Lincroft, NJ. Masonry contractor: Etter Mason Contractors, Howell, NJ.

Top An arched firebox opening, a raised hearth extension, and a herringbone panel add spice to this traditional fireplace. Randomly placed stone enhances the rustic used brick, recycled from a demolished warehouse. An oak mantel shelf, supported by corbeled brick, completes the effect. Designer and masonry contractor: Ottavio Rosati, Lockport, NY.

Bottom An arched opening adds drama to this large family room fireplace with a 42-inch firebox. The soldier course at the top balances the raised hearth, while the mottled brick give the fireplace a rustic effect. Masonry contractor: Etter Mason Contractors, Howell, NJ.

John Suhay

SCULPTURED BRICK FIREPLACES

For a fireplace that exemplifies both the art and craft of masonry, forget about finding the perfect painting to hang above the mantel and consider incorporating a brick sculpture instead. If you plan ahead, many brick manufacturers can arrange for a sculptor to create a design especially for your fireplace wall. Whether it contains abstract or naturalistic images, strongly modeled forms or delicate low-relief, a brick sculpture provides a unique and memorable focal point.

Allen Moran

John Suhay

Opposite Page A rural scene, complete with barn and cattails, is the subject of this 4-foot-by-5-foot custom carved brick mural. The entire project, including the hearth, uses bricks of shale native to Ohio. Sculptor: Allen Moran. Masonry contractor: Rodger Snyder, Nashport, OH.

Top This fireplace wall has a fireplace, entertainment center, and 6-foot-by-14-foot abstract brick sculpture. The brick includes extra-thick, modular-faced sculpted units. After the green brick were carved, the sculpture was taken apart, coated and fired to replicate the blended brick. Sculptor: Ken Williams, Williams Studios, Pueblo, CO. Architect: David Barber, Colorado Springs, CO. Masonry contractor: Virgil Reutter, Virgil Reutter Masonry, Pueblo, CO. Material supplier: Summit Brick & Tile Co., Pueblo, CO.

Bottom The focal point of this brick fireplace, which extends to a 16-foot cathedral ceiling, is a custom carved 4-foot-by-6-foot mural of an eagle catching its prey. The material is Autumn Blend Smooth Face Brick, which is also used on the matching raised hearth. Masonry contractor: Del Miller, West Holmes Masonry, Millersburg, OH. Material supplier: Bowerston Shale Company, Bowerston, OH.

13

John Suhay

Ken Williams

Kris King © 1994 Architectural Murals in Brick

Kris King © 1994 Architectural Murals in Brick

Opposite Page, Top This contemporary, Russian-style fireplace graces the showroom of Summit Brick & Tile Co. in Pueblo, CO. It has a 3-foot-by-6-foot-8-inch abstract mural sculpted by the artist who carved the company's name and logo on the exterior of the building. The brick was carved while soft, then fired, and installed. Sculptor: Ken Williams, Williams Studios, Pueblo, CO. Architect: Gary Trujillo and Bob Hart, Pueblo, CO. Masonry contractor: Benno Schmidt, Benno Schmidt Masonry, Pueblo West, CO. Material Supplier: Summit Brick & Tile Co., Pueblo, CO.

Opposite Page, Bottom This unique fireplace, which resembles a patchwork quilt, is made of manufactured brick and hand-carved, colored tile made from brick clay and installed in a random arrangement. The geometric design was carved on soft, unfired brick. It was then coated with a conventional ceramic glaze, for a glossy effect, or a colored clay for a matte finish, and then fired. Sculptor: Ken Williams and Judy Williams, Williams Studios, Pueblo, CO. Material supplier: Summit Brick & Tile Co., Pueblo, CO.

Top and Right This contemporary-style fireplace is highlighted by a hand-carved, site-specific mural. Entitled "Whales off Camano Island," the 4-foot-by-3-foot mural is carved in Carib/Economy Brick, laid with grey mortar, and framed with pool coping. Sculptors: Mara Smith and Kris King, Architectural Murals in Brick, Seattle, WA. Masonry contractor: Glenn Homfeld, Homfeld Masonry, Ferndale, WA.

Dirk Baker

Opposite Page A dramatic 4-foot-by-5-foot carved brick mural is the focal point of this contemporary fireplace. The deer were carved on soft bricks which then were fired and installed with colored mortar in this 10-foot-high fireplace. The distinctive color of the brick derives from the shale native to East Central Ohio. Sculptor: Allen Moran. Masonry contractor: Rodger Snyder, Nashport, OH.

Top "Whimsical" is a good adjective for this sculptured brick fireplace. Using raw terra cotta or high-fire stoneware bricks, the mason makes the initial design and then carves it into the finished product. Bricks are then hollowed out and numbered to be easily reassembled. Masonry contractor: Jerome Ferretti, Detroit, MI.

Randal Guida

STONE FIREPLACES

Depending on how it's handled, stone can fit the mood of any home. Whether you choose rounded river rocks laid up in their natural state, fieldstone split and shaped, or marble intricately carved and polished—a stone fireplace always is a unique design. With its wide range of colors, textures, and veining patterns, stone adapts to rustic or sophisticated, traditional or cutting-edge contemporary styles.

Cast stone, a fine-grained, architectural precast concrete that simulates limestone or sandstone, expands your options still further.

Randal Guda

Steve Cohan

Opposite Page Its central location makes this large fireplace with an Acucraft heat exchanger the focal point of the house. The block case and chimney are surrounded by a layer of central Minnesota fieldstone. Several large rocks were used, including one 32-inch-diameter, 175-pound boulder shown on the left. A stone grill and two Norway pine mantel shelves are highlights. Masonry contractor: Randal Guida, Randal Guida Masonry, Sunburg, MN.

Top This dramatic double fireplace is set between the living room and dining room. One side features an arched 4-inch inset area, with Juperano polished granite used for the surround, mantel shelf, and hearth. The firebox, of Pacific Clay firebrick set in a herringbone pattern, has side walls splayed 10 inches from the curved back wall. The other side features a 5-by-5-foot arched opening. Designer and masonry contractor: Rick Bibbero and Jamey DeMaria, Jamey DeMaria Masonry, Monterey, CA.

Bottom, Right Although this fireplace is more than 10 feet high, it has strong horizontal lines thanks to a hewn mantel shelf and shallow cut stones. Carefully recessed mortar creates a dry-stack look on this river rock fireplace, which has a large 5-foot-by-4-foot firebox. Masonry contractor: Steve Cohan, Hot Rock Masonry, Eastsound, WA.

Robyn Swenson

Leonard Roscoe

Opposite Page, Top, Left Flanked by two glass doors, this contemporary master bedroom fireplace is made of Pebble Beach golden granite, set in colored mortar. The 4-foot arched opening highlights the herringbone firebox. Two carved wood brackets support the chipped edge mantel shelf which is made of Juperano polished granite. Designer and masonry contractor: Rick Bebbero and Jamey DeMaria, Jamey DeMaria Masonry, Monterey, CA.

Opposite Page, Top, Right Natural Minnesota fieldstone was used to build this fireplace. An Acucraft heat exchanger and a heat vent made of vertical stones help to circulate heat efficiently. In a house handcrafted of logs, the natural log mantel shelf is a perfect fit. Masonry contractor: Craig Nagel, Craig Nagel Stoneworks, Pequot Lakes, MN.

Opposite Page, Bottom Minnesota fieldstone hand-picked from farm rock piles and gravel pits, Indiana limestone, and oak combine to create this fireplace wall. At the wall's center is an Acucraft heat exchanger with heat vents above it. The fireplace is flanked by wood storage areas, which are topped by oak built-in bookcases. Architect and masonry contractor: Leonard Roscoe, Swede's Concrete, Pierz, MN.

Top Nearly 7-feet tall, this Mediterranean-style fireplace is made of cast stone, a mixture of aggregate and portland cement. The technique has been used since the 1100s. The arch is a Tudor design, the twisted columns are Portuguese style, and the double ogee curves are medieval style. Material supplier: Classic Cast Stone of Dallas Inc., Garland, TX.

Edward J. Zywusko

Steve Cohan

Charlotte Brown

E. Hanuse

Opposite Page, Top This contemporary fireplace has a dark soapstone facing, white surround, and brick firebox. The raised bluestone hearth has a curved design. Architect: Gregory Rochlin, Cambridge, MA. Masonry contractor: Edward J. Zywusko, E-Z Masonry, Beverly, MA.

Opposite Page, Bottom, Left This three-sided, Rosin-style fireplace combines the rustic look of river rock from the Nooksack River with elegant cove molding at the ceiling. The raised hearth is also made of river rock. Masonry contractor: Steve Cohan, Hot Rock Masonry, Eastsound WA.

Opposite Page, Bottom, Right St. Genevieve stone is used for this traditional-style fireplace, which has a tapered fireplace. A 36-inch firebox, a raised hearth, and an 18-foot chimney highlight the piece. The mantel shelf, hearth, and reducers weigh more than 250 pounds apiece. Architect: Rick Raleigh, Raleigh Homes, Chesterfield, MO. Masonry contractor: John Spencer, John L. Spencer Brickwork Inc., St. Louis, MO.

Top and Bottom, Left River rock is used for the face and hearth of this fireplace, which features granite arches for the firebox and a wood storage area. A 12-foot cedar mantel shelf, carved by Native American artist Richard Krentz, lends a distinctive touch to this rustic fireplace. The painted carvings are reminiscent of designs found on traditional totem poles. The raised hearth and wood ceiling beam accent the strong horizontal lines. Masonry contractor: David Johnstone, David Johnstone Masonry & Design, Qualicum Beach, BC, Canada.

Edward Zywasko

Michael Eckerman

Opposite Page This rustic-style fireplace is contemporary in feel thanks to the clean geometry of its lines. The floor-to-ceiling fireplace is made of Rocky Mountain fieldstone, including the hearth. Recessed mortar joints emphasize the rustic effect of the irregular stones. Designer and masonry contractor: Edward J. Zywusko, E-Z Masonry, Beverly, MA.

Top, Left Copied from a late-17th-century French design, this 10-foot, 8-inch fireplace has a 47-inch opening and is made of cast stone. Material supplier: Classic Cast Stone of Dallas Inc., Garland, TX.

Top, Right The house surrounding this fireplace burned down, leaving only the fireplace. When the house was rebuilt, the fireplace was sandblasted. After an earthquake in 1989 destroyed both the fireplace and the house, the owner rebuilt everything. The free-standing stone and concrete masonry fireplace has a circular firebox, a modification of Rumford principles. The fireplace's water-washed flat stone came from Tehama County, California, and the river cobbles came from the Sierra and Arroyo Seco River. Designer and masonry contractor: Michael Eckerman, Santa Cruz, CA.

Charlotte Brown

Steve Cohan

Jim Cutting

Opposite Page, Top, Left A wood mantel shelf and raised hearth add horizontal lines to this otherwise vertical fireplace. Built of Penry limestone, this traditional-style fireplace has a segmented arch. Designer and masonry contractor: Brad Kelley, BKM Construction, Ostrander, OH.

Opposite Page, Top, Right The colors of two types of stone, St. Genevieve and buff Lannon stone, combine to give a warm look to this rustic fireplace. A 36-inch firebox with a shallow arch and a stone mantel shelf are featured on the fireplace, which tapers as it extends to a 14-foot vaulted ceiling. Architect: The Jones Company. Masonry contractor: John Spencer, John L. Spencer Brickwork Inc., St. Louis, MO.

Opposite Page, Bottom The focal point of this stone fireplace is a cast concrete plaque from a demolished bath house on Coney Island. The mason set the honey ledge rock in a spoke design to continue the nautical effect. Architect: Tom Kligerman, Ike & Kligerman, New York City, NY. Masonry contractor: Steve Cohan, Hot Rock Masonry, Eastsound, WA.

Top The arched opening and rounded tiles may be borrowed from traditional beehive fireplaces, but the tall plaster chimney gives this design a distinctive look. The Montana River rock, which contrasts starkly with the white plaster, has raked joints of a dark mortar for a dry-stacked look. The fireplace features an all-masonry firebox, a black granite hearth, and a plaster chimney. Architect: Jonathon Smith. Masonry contractor: Jim Cutting, Cutting Masonry, Somers, MT.

Michael Eckerman

Greg Mayer

Bob Neild

Opposite Page This freeform fireplace is large enough to support a collection of 4-foot ceramic pots. Made of Sierra cobbles with boulders for the seats, this fireplace has a 48-inch circular brick firebox, loosely based on Rumford principles. An upward sweep of the rock forms the support for the wood mantel shelf. Designer and masonry contractor: Michael Eckerman, Santa Cruz, CA.

Top Key coral, a fossilized coral from Florida City and mined from canals in Key West, is set in a coral-colored mortar made of white masonry cement and yellow coarse sand. When cut, the coral reveals entire cross sections of fan and brain coral, as well as shell, crab, and fish fossils. The main mantel shelf weighs 500 pounds. Architect: Jim Jennewein, Ruwle & Masters plus Jennewein, Tampa, FL. Masonry contractor: Frank Wright and Greg Mayer, Wright's Stone & Stucco, Tampa, FL.

Bottom, Left Straight lines, square angles, and a wood mantel shelf give this fireplace a contemporary look. But the rough textures of Tennessee River stone and Tennessee fieldstone make this fireplace, which features a 42-inch brick firebox and a 10-inch raised hearth, a bit rustic as well. Architect: Carol Hadley, Candler, NC. Masonry contractor: Bob Neild and Dale Bradley, Masonry Services Co./Quality Stone Masonry, Asheville, NC.

Wanda Miller

Steve Cohan

Opposite Page Traditional and contemporary design blend nicely in this rustic fireplace, which is flanked by a pair of split Palladian windows. The thin mortar joints between the Tennessee River stones give the appearance of dry-stacked masonry on this 7-foot, 6-inch-wide fireplace. The 42-inch firebox sits on a 12-inch raised hearth and is topped by a segmental arch and wood mantel shelf. Architect: Pete Green, The Green Company, Hendersonville, NC. Masonry contractor: Bob Neild and Steve Ballew, Quality Building Stone and Supply Inc., Fletcher, NC.

Top, Left This fireplace is built from Northshore Split Blue Limestone. The Romanesque segmented arch is built at the same proportion as the stone arch in the foyer, and

adds a traditional touch to the contemporary fireplace. Designer and masonry contractor: Brad Kelley, BKM Construction, Ostrander, OH.

Top, Right Limestone salvaged from a 100-year-old lime kiln is used for this dramatic, contemporary fireplace. The three-sided chimney, raised hearth and angled sidewalls are all accented by the wood mantel shelf. Architect: Roy Lundgren, Eastsound, WA. Masonry contractor: Steve Cohan, Hot Rock Masonry, Eastsound, WA.

Michael Eckerman

Michael Eckerman

Opposite Page This fireplace has a brick firebox and a surround of cast stone, a mixture of aggregate and portland cement pressed into molds to produce the look of cut limestone. The fireplace, installed with a hooded chimney, has a Tudor-style top combined with a simple surround. Material supplier: Classic Cast Stone of Dallas Inc., Garland, TX.

Top, Left and Right This air-circulating fireplace is a combination of river rock, brick, various precious stones, and pottery shards from a 1989 earthquake. The raised hearth is made of brick. Designer and masonry contractor: Michael Eckerman, Santa Cruz, CA.

Gerald Fransen

RUMFORD FIREPLACES

In the late 18th century, Count Rumford redesigned the conventional fireplace to make it a more efficient heat source. With taller, narrower openings and shallower, splayed fireboxes, Rumford fireplaces reflect more heat into the room. The energy concerns of recent years have renewed interest in Rumford's principles.

Rumford's design works by altering the proportions of the fireplace. It can be adapted to almost any style or material, as illustrated by the examples shown here.

K.L. Munson

Opposite Page This 48-inch-by-48-inch stone Rumford fireplace, which looks like it dates back to early American times, is made of granite blocks that were quarried from the home owner's property, some taken from ledge outcroppings. The granite is laid without visible mortar for a dry look. The fireplace has outside air intakes built into the brick firebox. Even the hand-hewn cherry mantel shelf is from a tree on the home owner's property. Masonry contractor: Karl L. Munson, Masonry Construction, Falls Village, CT.

Top, Left This charming corner Rumford fireplace is located in a bedroom above a kitchen that has a large cooking fireplace. Both fireplaces feed into a brick chimney with clay flue liners. The fireplace surround and hearth are made of marble. Designer and masonry contractor: Jim Buckley, Buckley Rumford Co., Port Townsend, WA.

Top, Right Located in the master bedroom, this rustic brick Rumford fireplace has a 24-inch arched opening and a simple mantel shelf. Masonry contractor: Etter Mason Contractors, Howell, NJ.

Bottom, Left A traditional Georgian-style wood mantel shelf tops off this 12-inch-deep Rumford fireplace, which was built within an existing gas fireplace opening and chimney in a 1920s home. The fireplace has a tile surround and hearth extension. Architect: Steve Copeland, Schooley-Caldwell Architects, Columbus, OH. Masonry contractor: Jim Buckley, Buckley Rumford Co, Port Townsend, WA.

Bob Bowen

Superior Clay

40

Gerald Fransen

Bob Bowen

Opposite Page, Top A classic Georgian mantel tops this 30-inch-by-30-inch-by-12-inch Rumford fireplace which has a slate surround and hearth extension. It is one of three Rumfords on three different levels which were built as part of a new addition to an existing home. Architect: Ray Studebaker, Francios, Bartholme & Studebaker Architects, Seattle, WA. Masonry contractor: Jim Buckley, Buckley Rumford Co., Port Townsend, WA, in conjunction with Masonry Contracting, Seattle, WA.

Opposite Page, Bottom This 48-inch traditional cooking fireplace with an iron crane looks like something out of the 18th century. The 16-inch-deep Rumford has a wood storage area and JenAir cooktop instead of a customary wood-fired bread oven. The firebox, with walls more than a foot thick, is built with solid handmade red brick laid in high lime mortar. The designer used handmade brick with grapevine joints for the exterior of the fireplace, as well as for the firebox. Designer and masonry contractor: Jim Buckley, Buckley Rumford Co., Port Townsend, WA.

Top Spectacular cherry woodwork, including columns and arches, frame this Rumford fireplace. Located in the family room, the design uses Stiles & Hart Boston City Hall Pavers for everything except the hearth, which is native Concord gray granite. The throat contains two 12-inch-by-16-inch flues and is connected to one of the six herringbone brick chimneys in the house. Architect: Johnathon Hall, Sherman-Greiner & Hall Ltd., Concord, NH. Masonry contractor: Gerald Fransen, Fransen & Father Masonry, Merrimack, NH.

Bottom, Left The combination of a Georgian-style mantel shelf with veined marble used on the surround and hearth extensions gives this Rumford fireplace a look of classic elegance. Architect: Ray Studebaker, Francios, Bartholme & Studebaker Architects, Seattle, WA. Masonry contractor: Jim Buckley, Buckley Rumford Co., Port Townsend, WA, in conjunction with Masonry Contracting, Seattle, WA.

Norbert Senf

MASONRY HEATERS

Extending the appeal of woodburning from the aesthetic to the practical, masonry heaters and stoves are an efficient, ecologically responsible way to heat homes. They burn less wood than conventional fireplaces or wood stoves, and use a massive masonry core to absorb and radiate heat. Derived from long-standing European tradition, masonry heaters are attracting new interest in America.

Whether they're faced with brick, stone, stucco, or ceramic tile, masonry heaters deliver their practical advantages with style.

Norbert Senf

Stretch Tenler

Jim Cutting

Norbert Senf

Opposite Page European in flavor, this contraflow heater is built around a "Heat-kit" core. It is faced with ⁵⁄₈-inch soapstone tile over clay brick and features chamfered corners and mitered joints. The primary heating source for a 2,500-square-foot house, the heater has a heated raised hearth and a bake oven in the rear. Designer and masonry contractor: Norbert Senf, Masonry Stove Builders, Shawville, QUE, Canada.

Top, Left Taking its inspiration from a Finnish fireplace and a Chinese kang, a brick platform warmed by a fire beneath, this brick masonry heater has a soapstone mantel shelf, bench and shelves. Supported by a concrete-block foundation, the unit includes a masonry heater in the living room, an oven and stove top in the kitchen, and a heated bench in between. The back of the heater is a bathroom wall. Designer: Albert Barden and Michael Rothschild. Masonry contractor: Albert Barden, Maine Wood Heat Co. Inc., Norridgewock, ME.

Top, Right This rustic masonry heater is a Finnish contraflow design with a firebrick interior and a multi-level exterior made of used bricks recycled from an old school house. A by-pass damper on the upper left corner of the front face provides quick start ups. Masonry contractor: Jim Cutting, Cutting Masonry, Somers, MT.

Bottom, Left With a brick and lime-sand plaster face, this masonry heater combines a contraflow heater core and a brick bake oven set above it. The stack bond brick and compound chamfered brick arch are cut from solid red firebrick and laid in a lime-sand mortar. The unit provides the primary heat for a 1,500-square-foot home. Designer and masonry contractor: Norbert Senf, Masonry Stove Builders, Shawville, QUE, Canada.

45

John B. Silverio

EnviroTech Radiant Fireplaces, division of Dietmeyer, Ward & Stroud Inc.

EnviroTech Radiant Fireplaces, division of Dietmeyer, Ward & Stroud Inc.

Opposite Page This dramatic, contemporary masonry heater combines soaring contemporary lines with the rustic texture of Martin Clay Brick and Old Abbey CSR. The Crossfire 2100 wood-burning design includes see-through twin doors. The twin brick columns, which join to form a splendid loft arch, have active flues. Architect and masonry contractor: John Steele, The Stoneworks, Campbellford, ONT. Canada.

Top, Left Used brick adds texture and surface interest to this double-sided masonry heater. The heater's two identical faces, one in the living room and one in the kitchen, are connected by the firebox. Architect: John B. Silverio, Chimney House Design, Lincolnville, ME. Masonry contractor: J. Patrick Manley, J. Patrick Manley Brick Stove Works, Washington, ME.

Top, Right Installed during a major renovation, this modular-core brick masonry heater is dramatically accented by the timber framing of a wood walking bridge that connects the upper floor rooms. Masonry contractor: Dietmeyer, Ward & Stroud Inc., Vashon Island, WA.

Bottom, Left This brick masonry heater contains a modular core designed for ease of construction. With a marble hearth in front and a built-in cookstove in the back, it supplies the heat for a 3,500-square-foot house. Architect: Lou Hillendahl, Vashon Island, WA. Masonry contractor: Dietmeyer, Ward & Stroud Inc., Vashon Island, WA.

D. Johnstone

EnviroTech Radiant Fireplace, division of Dietmeyer, Ward & Stroud Inc.

Opposite Page A hybrid between a conventional wood-burning fireplace and a masonry heater, this Moberg/Royal Crown design has a fireplace-styled masonry heater core system. The unit, which has large air-tight glass doors, is made of Montana fieldstone from the Crazy Mountains in Colorado. A hammered metal surround and a deep set wood mantel shelf highlight the fireplace. The back side contains wood storage, cleanouts, and air supply vents. Masonry contractor: Ron Pihl and Dale Hisler, Cornerstone Masonry. Core System: Walter Moberg, Firespaces Inc., Portland, OR.

Top Gray river rock adds a rustic texture to this masonry heater built, which is built around a refractory core and has a bake oven. Heater core designer: Ernst Heuft. Masonry contractor: David Johnstone, David Johnstone Masonry & Design, Qualicum Beach, BC, Canada.

Right This may look like a conventional stone fireplace, but it's actually a modular masonry heater faced with native Washington river rock in the living room and brick in the den. The stone is angled to meet the exposed-wood ceiling of this waterfront house. The brick side of the heater has its own bake oven. Masonry contractor: Thomas Stroud, Dietmeyer, Ward & Stroud Inc., Vashon Island, WA.

Kachelofen Unlimited

J.E. Frisch

Opposite Page Oversized ceramic tiles with an arched motif add drama to this Kachelofen-style tile heating stove. Made of firebrick materials and imported tiles, this stove has a large glass fire door. Designer and masonry contractor: Gunter Richter, Pacific Tile Stoves, Auburn, CA.

Top, Left Chocolate brown tiles and cement-based white stucco are used as facing materials on this free-form masonry heater. The heater combines a Kachelofen- and hypocaust-style fireplace with a warming oven and stairway. The fireplace has a second combustion chamber to increase heating efficiency. Designer and masonry contractor: Kachelòfen Unlimited, Williams, OR.

Top, Right Ceramic tile combine with stucco facing to produce this Kachelofen-style heater. The five-flue heater has a castable refractory core and a tile and stucco custom hearth on three sides. Designer and masonry contractor: J.E. Frisch, Lopez Quarries Masonry Heaters/ Firecrest Fireplace Co., Everett, WA.

EnviroTech Radiant Fireplace, division of Dietmeyer, Ward & Stroud, Inc.

Olenych Masonry, Inc.

Olenych Masonry, Inc.

Opposite Page This modular masonry heater is designed based on the grundofen style. Made of brick covered with plaster, the heater has a granite hearth and opens into the living room on one side and a lap pool on the other. A hand-built, wood-fired cookstove is at the base of the arched wood storage area. Architect: Myrvang Architects, Poulsbo, WA. Masonry contractor: Dietmeyer, Ward & Stroud Inc., Vashon Island, WA.

Top and Left White stucco covers the firebrick core and brick outer shell of this Finnish-style, down-drafting masonry heater. The heater's side panel, mantel shelf, and bench tops are made of soapstone. Glass doors on both sides allow the fire to be seen from both the dining room and living room. Masonry contractor: Olenych Masonry Inc., Bovina Center, NY.

Kerry Hill, Cross-Fire Heat Storage Systems Inc.

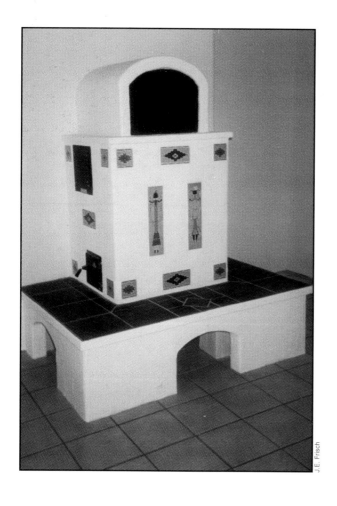

J.E. Frisch

EnviroTech Radiant Fireplace, division of Dietmeyer, Ward & Stroud, Inc.

EnviroTech Radiant Fireplace, division of Dietmeyer, Ward & Stroud, Inc.

Opposite Page, Left This grundofen-style masonry heater has a core that was imported from Europe. Firebrick is used on the interior and Southwest-style stucco and tile are on the exterior. Warming and bake ovens are on the side. Masonry contractor: J. E. Frisch, Lopez Quarries Masonry Heaters/Firecrest Fireplace Co. Everett, WA.

Opposite Page, Right Built of brick and faced with stucco, this gas-fired contraflow masonry heater has a modular precast refractory core that is thermostatically controlled. Masonry contractor: Steve Hodges Construction/Cross-Fire Heat Storage Systems Inc., Wainfleet, ONT, Canada.

Top, Left and Right Stucco and Mexican tile clad this contemporary Southwest-style masonry heater that also has a bake oven that is fired separately from the heater. Designer and masonry contractor: Dietmeyer, Ward & Stroud Inc., Vashon Island, WA.

Michael Eckerman

CHIMNEYS

If it's watertight, sturdily built, and properly sized, a chimney should function perfectly well. But as the hand-crafted product of a skilled mason, a chimney can make a strong design statement as well. Selecting a beautiful material, elaborating on the basic shape, and incorporating decorative patterns and accessories all can contribute to a chimney's visual impact. As the following examples show, many builders and owners are taking advantage of the chimney's potential as a major element in a home's exterior design.

Dean Ventola Architect

Gerald Fransen

Gerald Fransen

Gerald Fransen

Bob Neild

Opposite Page, Top This English-country style chimney is made of brick and block. The chimney's vertical position acts as an anchoring feature to the horizontal house and as a balancing accent feature to the front door's asymmetrical position. The chimney is attached to a brick, air-circulating fireplace. Architect: Dean Ventola, Dean Ventola Architect, Gaithersburg, MD. Masonry contractor: Milliner Construction, Frederick, MD.

Opposite Page, Left, Right and Bottom All these chimneys, which are on a single house, are made of Stiles & Hart Boston City Hall Pavers. Connected to Rumford-style fireplaces, with one chimney connected to three fireplaces, the Tudor-style chimneys have a recessed panel with three raised diamonds on the face and are topped with clay chimney pots. Architect: Johnathon Hall, Sherman-Greiner & Hall Ltd., Concord, NH. Masonry contractor: Gerald Fransen, Fransen & Father Masonry, Merrimack, NH.

Top A mixture of Tennessee River stone and Tennessee fieldstone adds a rustic texture to this sleek chimney, which is attached to a contemporary brick residence. Architect: Carol Hadley, Candler, NC. Masonry contractor: Bob Neild and Dale Bradley, Masonry Services Company/Quality Stone Masonry, Asheville, NC.

Jerry Rosslan

Jon Zachery

Michael Eckerman

Michael Eckerman

Michael Eckerman

Opposite Page, Top, Left and Right If this looks like something out of a Beatrice Potter fairy tale, there is a connection: These chimney pots are imported from England. This style, called "Lady McFadzen," is handcrafted from terra cotta and is shown here on a Victorian-style roof. Material supplier: The Northern Roof Tile Sales Co., Millgrove, ONT, Canada.

Opposite Page, Bottom, Left There is a traditional British flavor to this two-story chimney thanks to its clay pots and corbeled top. The chimney is made of Richards 1N91 Goshen Blend Brick, and the herringbone inlay is surrounded by a double rowlock arch with a limestone keystone. Masonry contractor: Tom Wilbers, Tom Wilbers Masonry, Jefferson City, MO. Material supplier: Midwest Block & Brick Inc., Jefferson City, MO.

Opposite page, Bottom, Right This contemporary residence echoes the work of late Victorian architects. The massive chimney, with its corbeled top and clay chimney pots, is typical of that style. The arched brick inset echoes the arched windows that surround it. Material supplier: Cherokee Sanford Brick, Sanford, NC.

This page A collage of materials, including Sierra River cobbles, large creek granite, red brick, and 1-inch-thick colored glass, combine to form this chimney. An infinity sign begins halfway up the chimney and twists to the chimney's top. Designer and masonry contractor: Michael Eckerman, Santa Cruz, CA.

Kris King ©1993, Architectural Murals in Brick

Kris King ©1993, Architectural Murals in Brick

Jon Zachery

Steven E. Dahill

D. Johnstone

Michael Eckerman

Opposite Page, Top, Left Inspired by Arts and Crafts-style bungalows with their signature pillars, this contemporary home combines modern fenestration with traditional masonry. The massive chimney, flanked by two overscaled windows, blends Penry Buff Limestone and North Shore Split Blue Limestone, which is also used for the bottom half of the porch's pillars. Designer and masonry contractor: Brad Kelley, BKM Construction, Ostrander, OH.

Opposite Page, Top, Middle and Right A 3-foot-by-6-foot mule deer mural is the focal point on this chimney. The mural, which was carved by hand, is made of colored mortar and leftover 4x4x8-inch and 8x8x4-inch Carib-colored brick from various jobs. The larger brick is used for the deep-cut areas of the mural. The colored mortar is carefully matched to the Carib-colored brick to avoid distraction. Designer: Mara Smith and Kris King, Architectural Murals in Brick, Seattle, WA. Masonry contractor: Ladd Masonry, Sanger, CA.

Opposite Page, Bottom The twin chimneys on this neo-Georgian house, with its broken pediment doorway, have corbeled tops ending in vaulted brick arches that seem to echo the semi-circular entry stairs. Material supplier: Cherokee Sanford Brick, Sanford, NC.

Top, Left Perhaps inspired by the raised hearths so popular on fireplaces, this exterior stone chimney turns the concept into a matching raised flower bed. The local river rock is used for this traditional stone chimney and riser and adds an interesting texture to the cedar shingle house. Masonry contractor: David Johnstone, David Johnstone Masonry & Design, Qualicum Beach, BC, Canada.

Top, Right These chimneys have identical caps, but are at different heights to accentuate the different heights of the two gables. A perfect finish for this neo-Victorian house, the chimneys are made of K-F Plymouth Blend cured black and red brick. Designer and masonry contractor: Steven E. Dahill, North East Masonry Associates, Maynard, MA.

Bottom, Left This chimney, which resembles a large ceramic pot, was built for the home of a potter It is made of river rock and includes the owner's pottery rejects and seconds. The chimney is attached to a modified Rumford fireplace. Designer and masonry contractor: Michael Eckerman, Santa Cruz, CA.

Clark's Masonry

Opposite Page, Top A combination of rustic stone and bold contemporary lines make this chimney the perfect finishing touch for a post-modern residence. Penry Buff Limestone and North Shore Split Blue Limestone are used on this traditional-style chimney, as well as on the entryway and front elevation. Designer and masonry contractor: Brad Kelley, BKM Construction, Ostrander, OH.

Opposite Page, Bottom, Left and Right Reminiscent of the English Arts and Crafts style, this decorative stucco chimney is trimmed with a wood crown and three-dimensional porcelain tiles, mounted as two bands below the crown. The tiles are fired to withstand the freeze-thaw cycle of the Northeast. Tile designer: Stephanie Mark, Pyridiam® Block & Tile, Stamford, CT. Architect: Shope, Reno, Wharton Architects, Greenwich, CT. Masonry contractor: Joe Ercoli, Hercules Tile Co., Danbury, CT.

Top, Left Made of Sun Set Stone, this chimney starts with a 6-foot base and tapers to 40 inches towards the top. The last three courses of stone are corbeled. The chimney is connected to a 42-inch firebox. Architect: John Callahan, Williams Construction Co. Inc., Nashua, NH. Masonry contractor: Larry Kostiew, KAP Masonry Contracting, Inc., East Hampstead, NH.

Top, Middle Made to suit any size flue, these terra cotta barley twist-style chimney pots are handcrafted in England. The spiral tops are reminiscent of Portuguese "Manueline" columns, and they sit on octagonal bases. Supplier: Northern Roof Tile Sales Co., Millgrove, ONT, Canada.

Top, Right These chimney pots look like they have been darkened by a century of wood smoke. Actually, they are new, handcrafted pots which were patterned and stained to match the original pots. Material supplier: The Northern Roof tile Sales Co. Millgrove, ONT, Canada.

Bottom, Left A bow-tie stepout design, in which every other brick is inverted, adds a textured focal point to this masonry chimney. Made of Tierra Brick, the chimney has a stack-bond design near the base, which echoes the walking course along the top. Architect: Jeff Clark. Masonry contractor: Jeff Clark and Jack Clark, Clark's Masonry, West Milton, OH.

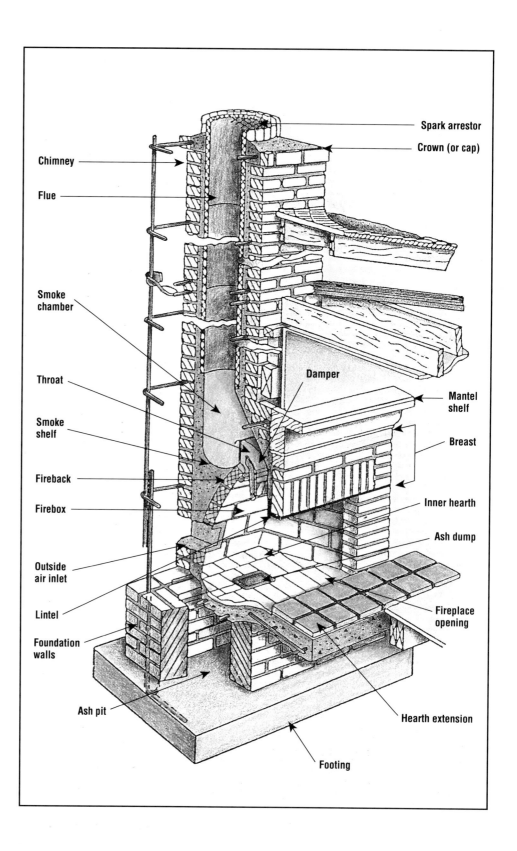

Spark arrestor

Crown (or cap)

Chimney

Flue

Smoke chamber

Throat

Damper

Mantel shelf

Smoke shelf

Breast

Fireback

Firebox

Inner hearth

Ash dump

Outside air inlet

Fireplace opening

Lintel

Foundation walls

Ash pit

Hearth extension

Footing

GLOSSARY

A Glossary of Chimney/Fireplace Terms

Fireplace components

Ash dump: The trap door to the ash pit.

Ash pit: An optional, noncombustible storage space into which the ashes are dumped so they don't have to be carried through the house.

Breast: Area above the fireplace opening and in front of the throat; also called the fireplace face.

Cleanout door: A metal frame and door built into the chimney to allow soot and ashes to be removed.

Damper: A device, usually extending the full width of the throat, used to regulate the draft from the firebox into the smoke chamber.

Fireback: The back wall of the firebox.

Firebox: Chamber where the fire is built. Usually constructed with firebrick, the chamber's side walls are splayed outward to radiate heat into the room.

Fireplace opening: The opening through which the fire is built and viewed. Its area determines flue size.

Hearth extension: Made of brick, tile, or other noncombustibles, extension is required (by most codes) to extend at least 8 inches on each side of the fireplace opening and 16 inches in front.

Inner hearth: Floor of the fireplace, usually made of fire-resistant brick.

Lintel: The reinforced masonry beam or steel angle above the fireplace opening that supports the decorative face of the fireplace.

Mantel shelf: Decorative shelf above the fireplace opening that holds ornaments.

Chimney components

Chimney: The vertical structure that carries combustion gases to the outside. Its height and flue size determine the proper draft through the fireplace.

Crown (or cap): Placed at the top of the chimney, the crown should be sloped away from the flue to prevent water from entering the joint between the flue and crown. It also improves the draft past the flue and flow of smoke exhaust.

Draft: Passage of air through the chimney.

Flue: Channel inside the chimney that carries smoke and gases to the outside. Usually made of $5/8$-inch-thick clay liners that conform to ASTM C 315, but also can be made of pumice, cementitious material, or metal. Flue area is generally $1/10$ that of the fireplace opening.

Foundation walls: Masonry or cast-in-place walls, usually unreinforced, designed to support the weight of the chimney and prevent its settling or tipping.

Outside air inlet: Reduces the amount of preheated room air used for combustion. An energy conservation feature, it is required for fireplaces located on an exterior wall.

Smoke chamber: Funnels smoke and gases from the fire into the chimney flue. Should be symmetrically shaped so the draft pulls evenly on the fire.

Smoke shelf: Prevents a downdraft from entering firebox and blowing smoke into the room. Also catches soot and keeps fireplace cleaner.

Spark arrestor: Screen on top of the flue that prevents sparks and other burning material from blowing out the chimney.

Throat: Slot directly above the firebox through which smoke and gases pass into the smoke chamber.

Wythe partition: A separating wythe of at least 4 inches placed between flues whenever more than one is contained in a chimney.

FLASHING CHIMNEYS PROPERLY

For adequate protection against water,
treat the base, cap, and roof intersection

BY KENNETH A. HOOKER

Because they are tall and frequently exposed on three or four sides, chimneys are especially vulnerable to water problems. Efflorescence, freeze-thaw damage and its attendant spalling, and sometimes even structural damage can occur unless appropriate steps are taken to prevent it. One such step is to install flashing at the base, roof intersection, and crown of masonry chimneys. Like all masonry flashing, chimney flashing is used either to close off openings and thus prevent water from entering or to direct water that enters a cavity back to the outside.

Configured and installed correctly, flashing at the roof prevents water absorbed by the masonry above the roofline from passing through to the masonry below.

Assess risk of damage

Different sources recommend different chimney flashing details. Some are simple, while others are more elaborate. To select the appropriate details for any project, the designer has to understand the flashing's function in each location and analyze the risk of water penetration and resultant damage.

Climate is one factor that contributes to that risk. A warm, dry climate offers less danger of water damage than a rainy one with frequent freeze-thaw cycles.

Consider, too, the chimney's design. A reinforced and fully grouted chimney designed to resist seismic loads will need less elaborate flashing than one with a cavity behind its brick veneer. Chimneys built of cored brick have a greater need for through-wall

flashings to prevent water from running through the cores, compared to those constructed of solid masonry units.

When in doubt, though, the designer and contractor should opt for more protection rather than less. Any time or effort saved by reducing the effectiveness of a flashing system could easily be wiped out in repair work later on.

Flash the chimney base

For exterior chimneys, built outside the building's exterior wall, base flashing is needed. This should be handled much like base flashing in a cavity wall. Install flashing in the joint between the foundation and the first course of masonry. The flashing should extend beyond the face of the foundation and turn down to form a drip. Inside the cavity, the flashing should be turned up for several inches, then embedded in a mortar bed joint in the backup wythe (Figure 1).

Roof intersection

Flashing at the intersection of the roof and the chimney prevents water from entering the gap between these elements and reaching the interior of the building. The flashing system directs any water that penetrates or runs down the face of the masonry back to the roof so it can drain away.

Designers should specify and detail the flashing system carefully, recognizing that the responsibility

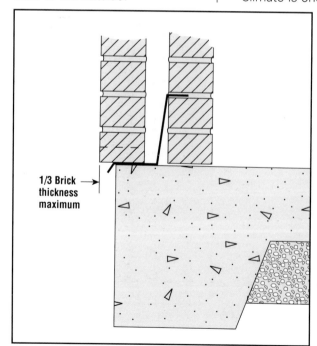

1/3 Brick thickness maximum

Figure 1. Exterior chimneys with masonry veneer backed by a cavity should have flashing between the foundation and the masonry facing.

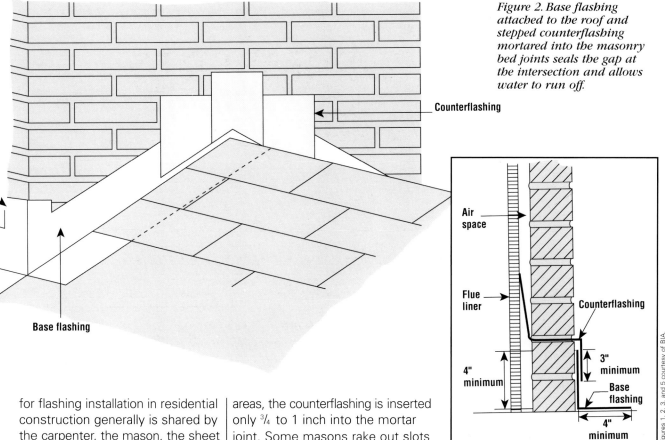

Base flashing

Counterflashing

Figure 2. Base flashing attached to the roof and stepped counterflashing mortared into the masonry bed joints seals the gap at the intersection and allows water to run off.

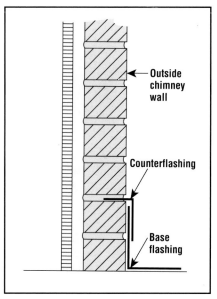

Air space

Flue liner

Counterflashing

4" minimum

3" minimum

Base flashing

4" minimum

Figures 1, 2, 3, and 5 courtesy of BIA.

Figure 3. Through-wall counterflashing prevents water absorbed above from passing into masonry below the roofline.

Outside chimney wall

Counterflashing

Base flashing

Figure 4. As an alternative to through-wall counterflashing at the roofline, a ¹/₂- to 1-inch deep slot can be raked out or sawcut in the bed joint. The counterflashing is then inserted in the slot and held in place with pointing mortar.

for flashing installation in residential construction generally is shared by the carpenter, the mason, the sheet metal worker, and the roofer.

Roof flashing is installed first, with the legs of the flashing extending at least 4 inches horizontally across the roof and 4 inches vertically up the face of the masonry. Seams between sections of flashing must be lapped at least 2 inches and thoroughly sealed. Counterflashing is then lapped vertically over the roof flashing, while its horizontal leg is inserted into mortar bed joints and mortared or caulked in place (Figure 2).

Some authorities, including the Brick Institute of America (BIA), recommend that the counterflashing be extended through the full depth of the bed joint and turned up behind the face brick (see Reference). To create this detail, the counterflashing is installed as the chimney is built. The horizontal leg creates a bond break at the bed joint (Figure 3).

In another method, common in warmer, drier climates and seismic areas, the counterflashing is inserted only ³/₄ to 1 inch into the mortar joint. Some masons rake out slots in the appropriate mortar joints when they're ready for tooling. Others wait until the mortar has hardened and then sawcut the slots for the flashing. Either way, the counterflashing gets inserted into the slot and is then held in firmly with pointing mortar or caulk (Figure 4).

Chimney crown flashing

A flashing system is needed at the chimney crown (or cap) to prevent water from entering the gap between the crown itself and the flue tile. Flashing also can provide a bond break between a brick chimney and a precast or cast-in-place concrete crown to relieve stresses due to differential movement in these dissimilar materials.

Here again, selecting an appropriate flashing detail depends on the design of the chimney and the potential for water damage. The reinforced and fully grouted chimneys built in seismic areas generally don't need crown flashing between the chimney and flue tile, because this space is filled with grout. However, flashing beneath the crown protects the walls if the crown should crack.

BIA recommends a detail that would provide maximum protection in the most severe exposures. Flashing directly below the crown extends beyond the chimney wall to form a drip. It passes through the chimney wall, then runs vertically along the outer face of the flue tile to the top of the flue. There it is folded over the exposed edge of the flue tile. The space between the crown and the flue tile is then filled with a compressible material, backer rod, and sealant (Figure 5).

A simpler, more commonly used detail handles the flashing in a similar way, except that the vertical leg ends even with the top of the chimney crown and is sealed there, rather than extending over the top of the flue liner.

Materials and workmanship

Once installed, flashing should remain serviceable for the life of the masonry. Deteriorated flashing can't provide effective protection against water problems, and repairing or replacing it later is difficult and expensive. Therefore, always consider quality and durability first when selecting flashing materials.

Both copper and stainless steel (ASTM A 167, Type 304) are durable, resist corrosion, and withstand the high temperatures present in chimneys. Aluminum, on the other hand, is damaged by the alkalies present in fresh mortar and thus should not be used.

Various plastic and composite flashing materials also are available, including some self-adhesive types that can simplify installation. Though somewhat easier to work with than metal flashings, these need to be evaluated carefully for durability, compatibility with other building materials, and performance at high temperatures. Consult the manufacturers for performance data and recommended applications.

Even well-designed flashing systems using high-quality materials are effective only when installed correctly. Flashings must be continuous, and any bends or breaks must be sealed completely. Flashing and counterflashing must be lapped enough to prevent water from getting behind the inner layer.

Proper attention to these details during design and construction can help minimize serious problems later on.

Reference

"Flashing Chimneys," *Engineering and Research Digest*, August 1992, Brick Institute of America, 11490 Commerce Park Dr., Reston, VA 22091.

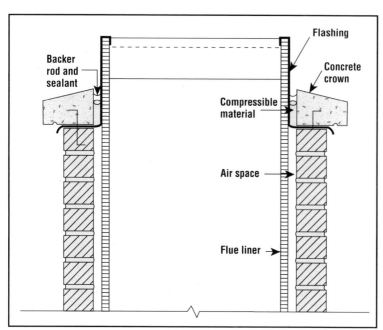

Figure 5. Flashing at the chimney crown should seal the gap between the flue liner and the chimney wall, while allowing for thermal expansion and shrinkage.

SELECTING FIREBOX MORTAR

For strength and heat resistance, adding fireclay isn't the answer. You want a refractory mortar, and here's why

BY KENNETH A. HOOKER

If you do some cursory research into fireplace design, you're likely to realize that some kind of special mortar is recommended for firebrick in the firebox. It's natural to assume that something other than the usual masonry mortar might be required for such a specialized application. If you consult several sources, however, you may find a confusing variety of recommendations. Even the model building codes are unclear on the subject.*

According to Jim Buckley, a Seattle-based designer and builder of Rumford-style fireplaces, most masonry fireboxes, unfortunately, are laid in ordinary portland cement mortar, sometimes with a little extra cement in it or with some fireclay added to make it "fireclay mortar" (one common recommendation).

Because few people use their fireplaces as a primary heat source (or even light fires in them very much), portland cement mortars often will work fine, at least in the short run. But after repeated cycles of exposure to extreme heat followed by cooling, portland cement mortars will deteriorate.

Adding fireclay to the mix sounds like a logical solution. After all, the firebrick are made of fireclay, so a "fireclay mortar" should be both compatible and heat-resistant. But fireclay isn't a cementitious material and doesn't bond to the brick. If the portland cement breaks down, there's nothing left to hold the firebox together.

What is refractory mortar?

In order to ensure good long-term performance of the installation, it's best to use a "refractory" mortar for both the firebrick lining the firebox and the clay flue lining in the chimney. Refractory mortars offer the same resistance to high temperatures as the firebrick and flue tiles.

Use refractory mortar for long-term durability when building a firebox. Joints between firebrick should be narrow, no more than $1/4$ inch and preferably $1/16$ inch or less.

Instead of calcium silicate, which serves as the binder in portland cement mortars, refractory mortars contain other compounds that bond with firebrick and don't deteriorate in high-temperature applications. In fact, they fuse to a ceramic and get stronger when heated. Two types of refractory mortar are common for use in fireplaces.

The first type uses sodium silicate as the binder. These refractory mortars are water-soluble and must meet "medium duty" standards according to ASTM C 199, "Pier Test for Refractory Mortar" (Ref. 1). They usually come premixed in buckets, and can be used for both firebrick and clay flue liners.

The second type contains calcium aluminate as the binder. Calcium aluminate mortars come preblended in bags or buckets, and are mixed with water on the job-site. Once cured, these mortars are non-water-soluble and highly resistant to acid attack, according to Bob Rucker, a manufacturer of fireplace and chimney materials and a member of the NFPA-211 Technical Committee of the National Fire Protection Association (NFPA).

Because calcium aluminate mortars are acid-resistant, the NFPA and others recommend their use in clay flues, where acidic water vapor released during combustion often condenses. The water and acid

*The National Fire Protection Association code is the strictest, calling for "refractory mortar (ASTM C-199, medium duty)" in Section 7-3.1.2. The BOCA National Building Code calls for "medium duty fireclay mortar" in Section 2402.2. The Uniform Building Code, Section 3707© just requires that "joints in firebrick shall not exceed $1/4$ inch."

Photos by Jim Buckley

Any voids in the joints should be filled after the firebrick are in position. With a water-soluble (sodium silicate type) premixed product, neatness isn't essential. Mortar smears will wash off easily.

After cleaning, the finished firebox looks neat. The mortar sets as it dries and will fuse to a ceramic when exposed to high temperatures.

can attack and eat away portland cement and other mortars, then leak out and soak the surrounding masonry.

Building with refractory mortar

During firebox construction, refractory mortars are handled differently than conventional mortars. That's because, to perform properly, the joints between firebrick must be narrow—no wider than 1/4 inch and preferably 1/16 to 1/8 inch.

Buckley prefers using the premixed, water-soluble type refractory mortars for fireboxes. They have a consistency similar to that of drywall joint compound, which makes creating thin joints fairly easy. And because these products do not set hydraulically (they gain strength by drying rather than by chemical cur-

ing), you needn't wet the firebrick before laying them.

Buckley recommends using a small, square margin trowel, because it fits better in the mortar bucket than a pointed bricklaying trowel. Butter a thin layer of refractory mortar on the firebrick, then lay the brick with a 1/16-inch joint, and scrape off the excess mortar.

Go back and add refractory mortar to fill any voids. Buckley says not to waste time trying to be neat. The mortar may get messy, but it's easy to clean up just by washing down the firebox when you're finished.

The Brick Institute of America (BIA) suggests another method for creating narrow firebox joints in its Technical Note 19A (Ref. 2). Mix the mortar to a somewhat soupier

consistency, then dip the head and bed surfaces of the unit into the mortar and immediately place it into position.

Clients who want all-masonry fireplaces should be able to enjoy all their benefits, including long-term durability. By specifying and properly installing firebrick with refractory mortar, you can ensure that they do.

References

1. ASTM C-199, "Pier Test for Refractory Mortar," American Society for Testing and Materials, 1916 Race St., Philadelphia, PA 19103.
2. "Residential Fireplaces Details and Construction," BIA *Technical Notes on Brick Construction*, Number 19A, Brick Institute of America, 11490 Commerce Park Dr., Reston, VA 22091

HOW TO CONSTRUCT A CHIMNEY CROWN

Make sure it allows for expansion and contraction and sheds water

BY CAROLYN SCHIERHORN

This steel crown form features a built-in drip edge and $\frac{1}{2}$ x $\frac{1}{2}$-inch support tabs in each inside corner. The tabs rest on the masonry, while the form itself abuts the outside edge of the masonry. Adjustable crown forms can fit any size chimney—up to the length of the form rails, which generally are 2 to 8 feet long; however, no more than two-thirds of the length of the form should extend beyond the chimney.

Whether made of precast or cast-in-place concrete, a properly constructed chimney crown (also called a cap or top plate) sheds water and seals the top of the chimney. By trapping air in the space between the flue liner and the masonry, the crown also enhances the chimney's insulation (except in areas governed by the Uniform Building Code, which requires this space to be grouted).

But much of the time, chimney crowns are poorly built, says Dale Deraps of Advanced Chimney Techniques in Jamestown, Mo. In fact, poor crown construction is a leading cause of chimney deterioration and failure.

Many crowns consist of a thin mortar wash that erodes quickly, shrinks, and cracks, causing moisture penetration. A large area of mortar, placed horizontally, will not resist weathering and temperature changes as well as concrete. In addition, crowns commonly end flush with the edge of the chimney, enabling water to run straight down the masonry.

Crowns sometimes butt up against the flue liner, failing to allow for its thermal expansion. Not only can moisture enter through this unsealed connection, but also vertical expansion can lift the crown, causing damage to the masonry courses below.

What's more, masons some-

times neglect to establish a bond break between the crown and masonry. Differential expansion will cause cracking and water penetration. And some crowns rest on combustible supports such as plywood or tar paper, which can burn and sag. Since plywood absorbs water, it also can expand and crack the crown.

73

Chimneys frequently suffer water damage, freeze-thaw erosion, spalling, and efflorescence as a result of faulty crown construction, keeping chimney repair specialists busy. "For lack of a good crown, I've taken large chimneys straight to the ground and rebuilt them," Deraps says. "These are $10,000 to $12,000 jobs."

Water penetration will shorten the life of masonry or steel fireboxes, which often require extensive repairs in less than 10 years, adds Jerry Isenhour of Concord, N.C.-based The Chimney Doctor Ltd., who is technical director of the National Chimney Sweep Guild (NCSG). Smoke chambers also are frequently damaged by water. "Water penetration will erode parging and wash out mortar joints," he says.

BIA guidelines

The Brick Institute of America (BIA), which receives numerous complaints about "disintegrating" brick near the top of chimneys, has issued the following guidelines for chimney crown construction (Ref. 1 and 2):

- Never use mortar as the crown material
- Make sure precast concrete crowns are at least 2 inches thick at the thinnest part

This steel crown form features integral clamps for fast and easy adjustment.

Integral fiber reinforcement may be added to the chimney crown concrete during mixing.

- Reinforce cast-in-place concrete crowns
- Make sure the crown extends at least 2½ inches beyond the outside chimney wall; a drip edge, or groove, should be incorporated on the underside of this overhang—at least 1 inch from the chimney wall
- Slope the crown downward from the flue liner to the edge of the chimney wall
- Don't let the crown touch the flue liner
- Use a sealant between the flue liner and the crown
- Maintain the required distance between the top of the installed crown and the top of the flue liner, as dictated by local building codes
- Make sure there is a bond break between the crown and the masonry to allow for differential expansion

Precast versus cast-in-place

Precast concrete crowns are easy to install and provide consistent quality, but they generally are used only in new construction or on smaller jobs, such as 16x16-inch chimneys.

Chimney repair work usually is done by specialists who typically are small contractors, notes NCSG

executive director John Bittner. The heavy weight of concrete (150 to 155 pounds per cubic foot) makes hoisting large precast crowns impractical. It's much easier to carry 50 to 70 pounds at a time and build a 450-pound crown in stages.

What's more, adjustable steel forms make it easier to construct cast-in-place crowns today. Masons traditionally have built wood forms by hand—a time-consuming process that must be repeated whenever the form wears out or the mason tackles a chimney of a different size. Steel forms require only half the setup time that wood forms do. Using C-clamps or built-in clamps, they can be adjusted in seconds to fit any size crown—up to the maximum length of the form.

Steel forms also last forever if properly maintained. Oil them before each use with a standard form oil. And clean the concrete residue off after each use.

Buying the right form

Steel form manufacturers generally offer form rails in 2- to 8-foot lengths, which refers to the maximum length of crown the form will create. Don't use a large form on a 16x16-inch chimney, where 4 or 5 feet might be sticking out and the

To construct the crown support grid, cut the ends of angle irons in half so they can lay flat on the masonry.

form will be out of balance. Follow this rule of thumb when buying a form: No more than two-thirds of the length of the form should extend beyond the chimney.

Another consideration when buying a form is how easily it can be attached to the chimney and stripped out after the concrete has set. One manufacturer produces a form with a small $1/2 \times 1/2$-inch tab in each corner that rests on top of the masonry, while the form itself abuts the outside edge of the masonry. This type of form is simple to install and can be stripped out easily because only the small tabs are covered by concrete.

A second type of steel form requires the contractor to strap angle irons or brackets to the chimney before positioning the form rails. This type may be more time-consuming to install.

A third type of form rests right on the masonry, allowing about $1/4$ inch around the chimney's perimeter to become embedded in concrete. This type may be harder to strip out unless a good release agent is used. Additionally, if the masonry isn't level, the form will wobble and the crown will have imperfections.

Also, look for a steel form with a welded-in drip edge to save setup time, Deraps suggests. It pro-

duces an accurate and consistent drip edge.

A chimney crown needs a drip edge so that water drips away from the chimney, not down its surface. Water can run horizontally, but it can't run horizontally and then back up again.

Creating the drip edge

Install the steel crown form according to manufacturer's directions. If the form doesn't have a built-in drip edge, you can create one by placing a bead of caulk on the form. Alternatively, some contractors create the groove by placing a cotton rope in the form, which gets stripped out later. The drip edge should be located at least 1 inch from the chimney wall on the underside of the crown.

Support system and bond break

Next, install the crown support system, which covers the open area between the flue or flues and the masonry and serves as a bridge

Photo shows components of chimney crown in place: Flat metal plates cover the grid and masonry, serving as a bond break and as support for the concrete; flues are wrapped in metal sleeves to allow for silicone expansion joints; and wire mesh reinforcement in the concrete inhibits cracking.

from masonry to masonry. If contractors were to pour concrete without this support, the whole chimney would become filled. The support system also establishes a bond break between the concrete and masonry. It's important to have a bond break because masonry and concrete expand and contract at different rates.

To construct the support system, use angle irons of the appropriate length, cutting the ends in half so they can lay flat on the masonry. With these angle supports, build a grid that goes around the flue liner and across the span of the chimney. Then lay flat metal plates on top of this grid. (Reinforced cement backing board may also be used, but don't use combustible materials such as plywood or tar paper.) Place tape around the perimeter to seal the plates to the form.

Also, wrap the flue liner with a compressible material to allow a $1/4$- to $3/8$-inch separation between the concrete and flue liner. "The tile needs to be able to move up and down slightly, as well as expand outward, so it doesn't crack the crown," Bittner says. Like the masonry and concrete, the flue liner and concrete have different coefficients of expansion.

One manufacturer recommends placing metal sleeves around the flue liner, which remain in place and allow room for the silicone expansion joint. But Isenhour prefers to use $1/4$-inch-thick ceramic wool. "It can be either stripped out and the space siliconed over, or left in and siliconed over; it has the necessary flexibility," he says.

Put in an expansion joint that will be flexible and hold the bond break $1/4$- to $3/8$-inch away from the flue. This expansion joint should be made of silicone sealant, which seals out water but allows some movement, and may be added when the concrete is cast.

Don't wrap tar paper around the

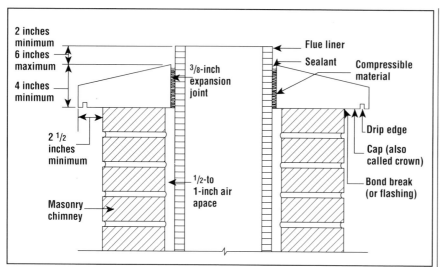

A chimney crown should slope downward from the flue and extend beyond the chimney wall.

flue liner to act as an expansion joint, as some masons do. While allowing for expansion up and down, it doesn't let the flue liner expand outward enough and will crack the crown.

Whether cast-in-place or precast, the crown should be seamless and finished so water will not collect on the top surface. The crown should be at least 4 inches thick to avoid premature cracking.

Make sure the flue liner extends at least 2 inches beyond the top of the chimney, but check local building codes for the requirements in your area. This extension permits attachment of a rain hood and keeps ice and snow that accumulates on the crown from dropping into the flue. To avoid excessive cooling and condensation, don't project the flue liner more than 6 inches above the crown.

For a cast-in-place concrete crown, one manufacturer recommends a rich concrete mix of 1 part portland cement, 2 parts concrete sand, and 2 parts coarse aggregate. It may also contain an integral water repellent.

Isenhour uses a batch mix that, per cubic foot, consists of 21 pounds portland cement, 42 pounds dry masonry sand, and 63 pounds of aggregate no larger than $1/4$ to $1/2$ -

inch. To this mixture, he adds 3 tablespoons of an air-entraining admixture.

Add reinforcement

A properly constructed chimney crown should not crack; but if it does, reinforcement can prevent the crack from expanding. If a hairline crack does develop, reinforcement can make the crack manageable; the crack can be ground out and caulked to prevent it from separating any further.

Integral fiber reinforcement may be added to the concrete during the mixing stage. One supplier advocates this type of reinforcement because it is three-dimensional, reinforcing up and down, as well as from side to side.

However, the most common method of reinforcement uses wire mesh, which should be placed mid-depth in the filled form. Be sure to select the right gauge and size. If the screen of the wire mesh is too small, bonding will not occur from one side of the mesh to the other. For chimneys, use at least a 1x1-inch mesh for optimum bonding through the holes.

When casting a crown in place, take the time to do the work accurately. Altering the crown after it is cast will make it look sloppy and fit poorly.

Fill the form with concrete, making sure that the wire mesh reinforcement, if used, is positioned properly. Don't let the mesh extend to the edge of the form or the outside surface. To prevent rust, there should be a 1-inch clearance between mesh and form and mesh and flue tile.

Cast the concrete so it slopes downward from the flue on all sides, shaping it with a wooden float. "You have to stay with it awhile and play with it," Isenhour points out. "You can't just dump it there and leave it."

Then Isenhour uses the rough side of a brick to smooth out rough spots and small surface cracks.

Finish the crown using magnesium and sponge floats to smooth the top and sides and a broom to make the texture more uniform. Tap the sides of the form gently with a hammer to release trapped air bubbles. A vibrator connected to the form also will force out the air bubbles.

Then cover the crown with plastic and allow the concrete to set overnight. Since weather conditions affect the curing rate of concrete, check the concrete for hardness before removing the forms.

To strip the form, follow manufacturer's directions. Be sure to scrape the form rails clean and oil them lightly for storage.

Use a tool called an edger to chamfer the edges of the concrete crown to the desired angle. Besides enhancing the crown's appearance, this increases its strength. Left sharp, the edges of a cured concrete crown may chip.

References
1. "Residential Chimneys Design and Construction," BIA *Technical Notes on Brick Construction*, Number 19B, Brick Institute of America, 11490 Commerce Park Dr., Reston, VA 22091.
2. "Proper Chimney Crowns," *Engineering and Research Digest*, BIA.

FILE: FIREPLACES

Distinctive, affordable fireplace designs
Ways to keep down the cost of masonry quality

BY KENNETH A. HOOKER

There's an elemental appeal to a fireplace that encourages both conviviality and quiet contemplation. And even without a practical need (since few use fireplaces for either cooking or primary heating), most prospective home buyers put a fireplace near the top of their wish lists. Recognizing this desire, builders are eager to provide a fireplace option, and the metal fireplace industry has promoted their product aggressively as a cheap and convenient way to do so.

But sacrificing the quality and durability of masonry isn't the only way to get an affordable fireplace. Here are some examples of modestly priced but handsome masonry fireplaces and some tips on keeping the cost of real masonry competitive with that of metal boxes.

Saving on labor costs

When designing a fireplace, remember that the cost of masonry resides largely in the skilled labor it requires, but don't forget that handcrafted uniqueness contributes to its value. The trick is to use labor effectively, saving steps that don't affect the fireplace's performance or appearance and concentrating craftsmanship where it will have the greatest visual impact. For instance:

- **Use the module.** Lay out the internal components as well as the fireplace face with the unit sizes in mind. Minimize the number of cuts needed and, whenever possible, use only whole and half units. (The "Toolbag Tip" on page 85 explains how this principle applies to flue and chimney construction.)

- **Reduce the components.** Take advantage of the modular firebox, throat, and flue component kits that are on the market (see *Masonry Construction*, February 1992, "Cost-effective Masonry Fireplaces Compete with Metal Boxes," and September 1993, "Building a Rumford Fireplace."). These kits greatly reduce the number of pieces, and thus the labor, required to build the internal parts of the fireplace.

- **Limit the size.** It may be obvious, but one way to reduce cost is to make the fireplace smaller. The material cost saved by using fewer units is minimal, but the reduction in labor can be more significant. A small fireplace with a brick surround and hearth may be just right for a room with an intimate scale. An imposing mantel or other wood trim, artwork, and accessories can add visual prominence to a small fireplace in a larger room. Another strategy for a big room is to build the fireplace with oversized brick or large pieces of stone. Just be sure the scale isn't jarring in a residential setting.

When considering fireplace size, remember that masonry fireplaces usually are described in therms of the size of the opening, while metal units are designated by the overall size of the cabinet. Thus a "42-inch" zero-clearance unit actually has a smaller opening and viewing area than a "30-inch" masonry fireplace.

Maximizing visual impact

The idea here is to focus on a masonry feature that takes advantage of the material's particular beauty or the mason's artistic skill to create a distinctive architectural or decorative statement.

- **Let the material star.** Because material is a relatively minor component of a masonry fireplace's cost, it pays to select a brick, block, or stone you love, even if the unit cost is on the high side. Handle it simply and use it sparingly if necessary, but let its color and texture make the impact.

- **Color the mortar.** The color of mortar greatly affects the masonry's appearance, and adding pigment to the mortar where it's visible won't add much to the cost. Coloring mortar to match or contrast with the units can make a significant decorative difference.

- **Feature the joints.** Freed from the need to resist wind-driven rain, mortar joints in interior masonry don't have to be concave-tooled to perform. Raked, flush, struck, or weeping mortar joints can add distinction to a fireplace face.

- **Alter the bond pattern.** Use rowlocks or soldiers for one course; project or recess some units or courses; or include a small panel of stack bond. If used sparingly, these and other simple techniques may not be prohibitively expensive.

By exercising imagination and common sense, designers and masons can offer their clients the quality masonry fireplace they want at a price they can afford.

BUILDING A RUMFORD FIREPLACE

Easy to construct, this energy-efficient tall and shallow fireplace is enjoying renewed popularity

BY JIM BUCKLEY

Mark Boisclair

Built by Jim Buckley, this tall and shallow Rumford has a straight back and rounded breast.

Rumford fireplaces are more popular now than at any time since 1850. Their traditional proportions look appropriate in homes with higher ceilings, which are growing in popularity. And their legendary heating efficiency attracts builders who are concerned with air quality. Over the past four years, U.S. building codes have been changed, where necessary, to permit these tall and shallow fireplaces.

Inventor Count Rumford, an expert on the nature of heat, published essays on fireplace construction in the 1790s. Although born Benjamin Thompson in Woburn, Mass., he was a loyalist who fled with the British in 1776 and conducted most of his fireplace research in England. He spent much of his life as an employee of the Bavarian government, which gave him the title "Count of the Holy Roman Empire."

Count Rumford understood that the only useful heat generated by a fireplace is radiant heat. So he designed a fireplace with a tall, wide opening; a very shallow firebox; and widely splayed covings, or jambs, to reflect as much radiant heat into the room as possible.

Intuitively understanding fluid dynamics, Count Rumford also streamlined the throat, or in his words, "rounded off the breast" in order to "remove those local hindrances which forcibly prevent the smoke from following its natural tendency to go up the chimney." He essentially created a venturi that, like an inverted carburetor, shot the smoke and air up through the throat and into the receiving smoke chamber.

Unfortunately, many fireplace designers and builders since Count Rumford's time have mis-interpreted his ideas and modified his designs. Some have failed to streamline the throat, for example. Indeed, the most popular 20th century book on Rumford fireplaces is Vrest Orton's *The Forgotten Art of Building a Good Fireplace*, now in its 23rd edition, which seems to combine the worst of the 18th and 19th century myths and inter-pretations.

But luckily, Rumford's essays on fireplaces, although out of print, are still readily available in libraries. The easiest to obtain is *The Collected Works of Count Rumford*, edited by Sanborn Brown (See Ref. 1).

In fact, Count Rumford may not have known how ingenious his "rounded breast" really was. Testing a Rumford at a brick manu-facturing plant, we wanted to see if the flow through the throat is laminar—that is, with the air and combustion gases in layers rather than mixed together. So we placed two thermocouples at the narrow-est part of the throat —one near the curved breast and one a couple of inches farther back near the fire-back. To our amazement, with an established 1,700° F fire, we record-ed only 75° F near the curved breast and 730° F near the fireback.

That proved that the flow is laminar: The room air coming in over the fire doesn't mix with the hot products of combustion; rather, it acts like an invis-ible glass door, keeping the smoke behind it, as they both go up through the throat together.

This revelation has far-reaching implications. Most engineers who are trying to come up with clean-burning designs to meet EPA emission stan-dards assume it can't be done with an open fireplace because, they say, the excess air mixes with and cools the gases too much to achieve secondary combustion.

What we've found is that the excess air does not mix turbu-lently with the products of com-bustion in a Rumford fireplace with a streamlined throat. Instead, the products of combustion stay iso-lated and hot behind the clean room air. And since a Rumford is tall, the gases driven off the fire stay hot for a long time— long

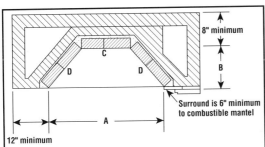

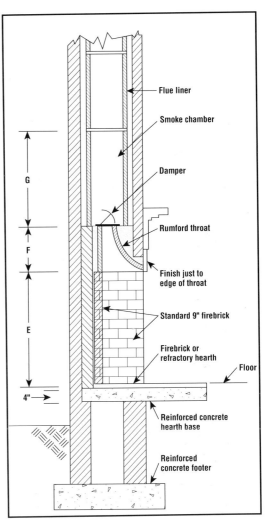

Flue liner

Smoke chamber

Damper

Rumford throat

Finish just to edge of throat

Standard 9" firebrick

Firebrick or refractory hearth

Floor

Reinforced concrete hearth base

Reinforced concrete footer

8" minimum

Surround is 6" minimum to combustible mantel

12" minimum

RUMFORD FIREPLACE DIMENSIONS

Fireplace Size	Throat (A x F)	Damper (Frame)	Smoke Chamber (Base x G)	Flue Tile	Other Dimensions						
					A	B	C	D	E	F	G
24" wide	24"x 2"	4"x16"	8.5"x18"x24"	8.5"x13"	24"	12"	13.5"	13.5"	24"- 28"	12"	24"
30" wide	30"x12"	9"x24"	13"x27"x30"	13"x13"	30"	12"	13.5"	15"	28"- 32"	12"	30"
36" wide	36"x14"	9"x24"	13"x27"x30"	13"x13"	36"	14"	13.5"	18"	32"- 38"	14"	30"
42" wide	42"x15"	9"x30"	13"x34"x30"	13"x18"	42"	15"	15"	21"	38"- 42"	15"	30"
48" wide	48"x16"	9"x30"	16"x34"x30"	16"x20"	48"	16"	18"	22.5"	42"- 48"	16"	30"

Diagrams and table show dimensions of Rumford fireplace components

Build the Rumford firebox with 9-inch standard firebrick; then set the curved Rumford throat in the refractory mortar on top of the firebox.

enough to attain secondary combustion. (Emission tests are now being conducted on Rumford fireplaces.)

Straight fireback advantage

Used to building modern fireplaces, most masons have trouble believing a Rumford will draw until they see it happen. The rules are different. In a modern fireplace, the fireback usually is sloped or rolled forward, casting the products of combustion forward. The incoming room air spills over the sharp edge of a steel lintel and mixes turbulently with the smoke.

Most masons assert that you need to "cross over" or drop the lintel about 8 or 9 inches below the damper to create a pocket for this smoke and allow the incoming room air to "roll"; if you don't, the fireplace will smoke, they argue.

Of course, inefficiently turbulent smoke and air need a huge throat to get through. But by keeping the fireback straight and rounding the breast to achieve streamlined air flow, we can build Rumford fireplaces with throats less than half the size of a modern fireplace and with openings almost a foot taller. No wonder Rumfords are more efficient. They radiate more heat and waste less heated room air.

Here's how to build a Rumford fireplace using a rounded fireclay throat and a two-piece smoke chamber:

Firebox

Build the Rumford firebox using standard 9-inch firebrick and refractory mortar, following the dimensions shown in the accompanying table and diagram. Keep the joints ⅛ inch or less. Fill any voids, and wash the firebox with a sponge and plain water.

The firebox must be backed up with solid concrete masonry units, so that the firebox walls are at least 8 inches thick. Fill the space between the firebrick and the concrete block with ordinary mortar.

Rumford fireplaces usually are about as tall as they are wide; however, lowering the height by a few inches can improve the draw. This is especially helpful in larger Rumfords because homeowners tend to build fires too small for the size of the fireplace.

Build the firebox as tall as the opening will be, and then build the fireback up another three courses. The covings will have to be built

Set the smoke chamber over the damper, making sure the damper will open and close freely.

up to meet the rounded Rumford throat but only after the throat has been set in place.

Throat

Set a prefabricated, one-piece curved Rumford throat in fireclay mortar on top of the firebox. These throats come in 24-, 30-, 36-, 42-, and 48-inch widths.

Pack the area between the throat and the surround masonry solid with ordinary mortar as you

Lay surrounding masonry at least 4 inches thick around the smoke chamber.

lay up masonry courses to the top of the throat. Although the throat is designed to carry the load, for an extra margin of safety, place a length of rebar in the first mortar joint above the front edge of the throat, which is 1½ inches thick.

Finish the firebox by building the curved covings up to meet the curved throat as high as the fireback and the top of the throat. Fill in the space between the firebrick and the throat with fireclay mortar.

Lay the surrounding masonry up to the top of the throat and the fireback to create a platform above the hearth on which to set the damper and smoke chamber.

Damper

Set the flat cast-iron damper over the opening left by the throat and the firebrick back. This damper should be set in a bed of wet mortar, but not restricted by any additional masonry laid around it. Make sure the valve plate is free to open. Close the valve.

Smoke chamber

Set the smoke chamber over the damper, making sure that the damper is free to open. The smoke

Flat cast-iron damper should be set over opening left by throat and fireplace back; make sure valve plate is free to open.

chamber may be shifted to one side or the other, forward or backward, or leaned to line up with the chimney so long as the damper valve opens without striking the inside of the smoke chamber.

If installing a two-piece smoke chamber, fill the joints between the two halves with fireclay mortar. Lay up the surrounding masonry at least 4 inches thick around the smoke chamber.

Now you're ready to set the first flue tile and continue the chimney just as you would any masonry chimney.

The surround

Finish the surround (the area about 6 inches wide around the fireplace opening) with plaster or a relatively thin material such as marble, slate, or tile. Adding a brick or stone facing that projects into the room 4 inches or more interrupts the line of the coving and makes the fireplace unnecessarily deep. Traditionally, Rumford fireplace surrounds were plastered and often painted black.

At the top of the fireplace opening, place the finish material just low enough to cover the edge of the throat, but maintain the line of the streamlined throat. This curve is like the leading edge of an airplane wing. Don't ruin the air flow by dropping a header several inches below the opening. Again, because it is difficult to maintain the streamlining, try to avoid a brick surround that would require an angle lintel to support the header.

References

1. *The Collected Works of Count Rumford*, volume 2, edited by Sanborn Brown, Harvard Press, 1969.
2. *The Forgotten Art of Building a Good Fireplace*, by Vrest Orton, Yankee Press, Dublin, N.H., 1969.

Jim Buckley is president of Buckley Rumford Fireplace Co. in Seattle.

The diagrams and all but the first photo were provided by Superior Clay.

CAN WOOD BURN CLEAN?

Initial results of masonry heater and fireplace tests suggest it can

BY KENNETH A. HOOKER

Searching for alternative fuel sources during the energy crisis in the 1970s, many Americans rediscovered wood. A plentiful, renewable resource, wood offered the additional appeal of self-sufficiency to individuals wary of relying on foreign oil or even regional utility companies for the power to heat their homes. Woodstove sales increased dramatically, especially in rural areas of New England and the Northwest. With the increase in wood burning came new concerns about the impact of wood-smoke emissions on air quality.

Woodstoves, when used as the primary residential heat source, are burned continuously throughout the heating season. And because of both design flaws and their owners' poor burning habits, metal woodstoves manufactured in the 1970s contributed strongly to air pollution in some areas.

Conventional masonry fireplaces, on the other hand, were not viewed as a significant source of air pollution. Most are used infrequently, for only a few hours at a time. Their primary appeal is aesthetic and, although some produce more usable heat than others, they are neither designed nor used to heat homes.

Masonry heaters are used for residential heating, but rely on the thermal mass of masonry to store and radiate the heat generated by one or two brief but intense fires a day. Their demonstrated combustion

Emissions test results led to EPA approval of wood-burning masonry heaters such as this Grundofen-style unit, for use in areas seeking to reduce air pollution

efficiency, as well as considerable European test data, suggest that masonry heaters also add little to air pollution levels.

But even though environmental concerns focused initially on woodstove emissions, these other wood-burning appliances also have come under scrutiny.

Regulatory pressures

Under pressure from environmental groups, the Environmental Protection Agency (EPA) began in 1986 to collect data on the combustion efficiency of woodstoves and on the characteristics of their emissions. EPA started looking at the amount of potentially harmful material woodstoves release into the atmosphere, including emissions of carbon monoxide (CO), volatile organic compounds (VOC), and particulate matter (PM).

The agency developed guidelines and standards for woodstove emissions, based on the results of tests performed according to specific laboratory procedures. Stove manufacturers were required to have their units tested, and those that passed were listed as "EPA-certified" appliances. After February 26, 1988, only EPA-certified stoves could be sold.

These regulations apply only to heating appliances that weigh no more than 800 kilograms and burn with an air-to-fuel ratio no greater than 35:1. Other units are referred to as "non-affected facilities." Because of their weight, virtually all masonry fireplaces or heaters built on-site are "non-affected."

This does not mean they are prohibited by EPA, only that they fall outside the category defined for certified stoves.

However, the terminology caused confusion when state and local governments, especially in the West, began formulating air pollution abatement regulations. Some of the proposed regulations allowed only EPA-certified wood-burning appliances, effectively banning both conventional masonry fireplaces and masonry heaters. Masonry advocates objected; fireplace builders and materials suppliers asserted that fireplaces have little impact on air quality, and heater builders insisted their units were at least as clean as certified woodstoves. While lobbying for regulatory changes, they soon realized they needed acceptable test data to support their position. In 1989, they began working on a research program to provide it.

Test program development

An initial test program, funded jointly by the Wood Heating Alliance (now Hearth Products Association), the Brick Institute of America (BIA), and the Masonry Heaters Association (MHA), was conducted by Dr. Dennis Jaasma at Virginia Polytechnic Institute. Jaasma tested emissions from traditional fireplaces, factory-built fireplaces, and two types of masonry heaters, using laboratory procedures adapted from EPA woodstove test methods.

Though the masonry heater test results were promising, it was clear that testing normally site-built fireplaces and heaters in the laboratory posed problems. For one thing, the dressed lumber prescribed as fuel in the test method, as well as the required "fueling protocol," bore little resemblance to the way fireplaces and heaters are used in the real world.

For reasons of economy and practicality, sponsors wanted a test that could be performed in the field, where units were fully installed and functioning normally. It was important to generate data that could be compared with data from EPA-method stove tests, but at the same time reflected the differences in how heaters and fireplaces are used. Furthermore, EPA was already moving toward field testing as a basis for certifying woodstoves.

The late Dr. Stockton G. (Skip) Barnett, of OMNI Environmental Services Inc. (now Scientific Applications International Corp.) in Beaverton, Ore., had spent several years developing such a test, using a unit called the Automated Woodstove Emissions Sampler or AWES.

Beginning in 1991, MHA engaged OMNI to perform field tests on several types of masonry heaters. The Western States Clay Products Association sponsored testing of conventional fireplaces. After an initial test, one fireplace was then retrofitted with a Rosin-style firebox and retested. Each unit was tested for one or two weeks.

Homeowners were given no special instructions, only told to operate their heaters or fireplaces as they normally would. They were to burn cordwood, not dressed lumber as prescribed for lab testing. OMNI provided the fuel, in order to control its moisture content, one variable that is known to affect emission levels.

OMNI also deviated from the EPA test method by reporting CO, VOC, and PM emissions in average daily grams per hour rather than in average grams per hour. These numbers are derived by averaging the actual emissions measured from 3 to 4 hours of burning over a 24-hour heating period. Although an emission rate expressed in grams per hour makes sense for wood stoves that burn continuously, the average daily grams per hour numbers more realistically estimate the environmental impact of heaters and fireplaces that burn only a few hours a day.

Another ongoing test program is being conducted by Jerry Frisch, a fireplace and heater builder with Everett, Wash.-based Lopez Quarries, and Norbert Senf of Masonry Stove Builders, Shawville, Quebec. Frisch uses a Condar dilution tunnel designed by Skip Barnett to test emissions in his laboratory, but approximates field conditions by using cordwood and field-style fueling protocols.

While testing a variety of masonry heater designs and Rosin-style fireplaces, Frisch has experimented with different fire-building techniques and methods of introducing combustion air. By studying the effects of these variables on emission levels, he is seeking ways to fine-tune his own designs to improve their performance. He also can instruct his customers on ways to fire their units with the least environmental impact.

Promising results

These emission studies have already shown positive results. The OMNI masonry heater tests confirmed the claim of heater advocates that these units are both clean and efficient. The results for the five heater types showed particulate matter emissions that rounded to 2.8 grams per kilogram (g/kg) of dry fuel burned. This number is nearly 90% lower than conventional metal woodstoves and much lower than EPA-certified woodstoves, which generally field-test at 7 to 8 g/kg. One Grundofen-style heater tested at only 1.36 grams per kilogram.*

After auditing these results, EPA approved the AWES field test method as a way to determine compliance with its emission standards. This decision allowed masonry heaters to be included in the federal Best Available Control Method (BACM) guidelines. EPA and local air-quality authorities use the BACM document when making decisions as to what pollution sources will be allowed in environmentally sensitive areas.

OMNI's fireplace tests showed reduced emissions when fireplaces were retrofitted with Rosin-style firebacks. Although further testing is needed, these findings suggest that modifying the design of masonry fireplaces can affect how cleanly they burn. Further work in this area, combined with research like Frisch's into firing methods, could well help bolster the competitive market position of masonry fireplaces as environmental regulations become more stringent.

---

*Masonry heater emissions stated in g/kg of fuel burned correlate closely with average daily grams per hour. Test reports give g/kg numbers to allow easy comparison with woodstove emission standards.

HOW AWES FIELD TESTING WORKS

The Automated Woodstove Emissions Sampler (AWES) system used in the OMNI field testing program draws samples of flue gases through a stainless steel probe at a predetermined rate, then passes them through a series of filters and sensors. Each filter is designed to trap or measure a particular component of the flue gas: an EPA Method 5-type filter collects particulate matter; a sorbent resin trap collects semi-volatile hydrocarbons; and a silica-gel trap removes water vapor.

Flue gas oxygen concentrations, used to determine flue gas volume, are measured by an electrochemical cell.

Throughout the test, a personal computer programmed with specialized software controls and monitors the operation of the test equipment, while logging and storing test data.

After the sampling period, the filters and traps, and any hardware that was in the sample stream, are removed from the test site and returned to the laboratory for analysis. The analysis reveals the amount and composition of particulate matter, the amount of carbon monoxide, and the amount and composition of volatile organic compounds collected during the sampling period.

Western States Clay Products Association

A personal computer controls and monitors the sensitive sampling equipment used to analyze emissions from the fireplace in this field test.

TOOLBAG TIP

The world's best fire

Though this is not strictly a masonry tip, fireplace masons might pass it along to their customers.

The greatest volume of smoke and particulate pollution from a wood fire occurs during a cold start-up. Wood fires lit from the bottom in a conventional manner promote a dirty burn and waste a large amount of potential heat in the form of unburned gases.

A clean and efficient method for kindling a fire is a top burn. This ancient European technique places the largest wood at the bottom in a criss-cross crib fashion.

1. Start with dry, well-seasoned split firewood and kindling. The wood will show radial cracks at the ends and sound like bowling pins when beaten together.

2. Lay the bottom layer using three pieces of split hardwood 5 to 6 inches thick, placed front to back. A fireplace grate isn't necessary with this method; logs burn best in contact with hot firebrick in a bed of wood ashes.

3. Lay the second layer using three pieces 3 to 5 inches thick, placed side to side. Criss-cross successive layers, decreasing the size each time until the pieces are about 1 inch thick.

4. Now alternate two or three layers of split softwood (spruce, pine, etc.) until the pieces are pencil thick.

5. Place a small piece of newspaper on top and light.

When the top burn fire is lit, the flames are always above the fuel load. The smoke and flammable gas from each tier of wood will always travel up through the flame and burn, thereby reducing particulate pollution and unburned fuel. A top kindling fire also produces large and less compacted glowing coals, providing long-lasting radiant heat.

A top burn fire laid with seasoned hardwood to a height of 18 to 24 inches will burn about 4 hours without adding more wood.
—*Fred Schukal and Chris Pryor, Sleepy Hollow Chimney Supply Ltd., Brentwood, N.Y.*